The JESUS PEOPLE Movement is a spontaneous work of God among the youth of America — and sprang up, seemingly by itself, in all corners of the country — *at the same time.* It is clearly directed by the Holy Spirit. Unquestionably, *the leader is Jesus Christ.*

Jesus People

By Duane Pederson
with Bob Owen

A Division of G/L Publications
Glendale, California, U.S.A.

First Printing — May 1971
Second Printing — July 1971
Third Printing — August 1971
Fourth Printing — August 1971

JESUS PEOPLE

Published by
Regal Books Division, G/L Publications
Glendale, California 91209 U.S.A.

ISBN 0-8307-0140-0

CONTENTS

CHAPTER ONE

God! What's Wrong?

I looked around me. Hollywood Blvd. was the same as I had remembered it. Nothing much had changed. Perhaps there were more people with long hair. More sandals and bare feet. More girls—and guys, too—selling themselves.

But there was something different. Everywhere I looked there were the underground papers: preaching revolution, sex, drugs, everything. I knew something was missing. Then I knew—there were no underground papers preaching the truth. Not a single one.

And I said, "God! What's wrong with us Christians?" I knew that one of the most effective media to communicate thoughts is the newspaper, and we weren't doing it.

I said, "Jesus, if You'll give me the means with which to do it, I'll put out a newspaper telling people about You."

Three days later I had the first copy out. And passed out all 10 thousand of them on the street myself . . . .

The shy, stuttering farm boy from Hastings, Minnesota that I had been just a few years before would have never ventured such a daring step of faith. The difference, I realized, was the power of Jesus Christ in my life . . .

Grade school to me was a world of fantasy. Totally unable to communicate because of my terrible stammer, I lived in a world apart. I had few friends, mainly the ones I made up in my dream world. And if elementary school had been rough, high school was one continual nightmare.

I was introverted, terribly insecure, trying to find my identity. College was much the same, only more so.

One night at a party, on an impulse, I made a rash statement that began to change my life. I was standing on the edge of a group of people who were talking about the upcoming play.

I cleared my throat and spoke nervously to a girl I was next to. "I . . . I . . . I'm g-g-going t-t-t-o try out for t-t-t-he p-p-p-play."

She laughed. "Duane, don't be ridiculous. You can't be in the play. You stutter!"

My face turned red as she and the others joined in the fun. I turned and slunk to my room in the dorm. I felt as if a rusty dagger had just ripped my heart out. All my life I had been laughed at. Now, a grown man, it was more than I could bear.

Somehow I got my hands on a copy of the play, then worked for hours memorizing portions of it. When I went to bed that night I was determined to make a showing the next day. There was hardly a chance in a million, I told myself, that I could succeed, but it would not be because I had not tried.

So when the try-outs were held . . . I was there. Several of the popular fellows auditioned, then I approached the director. "I'd like to try out," I said. Since I had practiced this line over and over again, I said it perfectly.

"Alright," he said. "Which part?"

"The lead."

I ignored the gasp of surprise that echoed in the room, and he apparently did not hear it.

"Okay, Duane. Here's a script. Read a few lines."

"I don't need it," I said. And I stepped to the center of the stage and did a portion of the play. From memory. I had chosen a portion that required me to yell and scream at my mother.

When I finished he said, "That's fine. Now do another part."

Again I refused the script, this time doing a scene in which I whispered to my girl friend across the stage. I had planned it this way, because I knew that I could either yell or whisper and not stutter.

Coupled with the fact that I had memorized these two scenes, I was able to do them both perfectly.

He said, "Thank you, Duane." And I thought that would be the end of it.

But the next day I was walking down the hall between classes and saw a bunch of people at the bulletin board. They were pointing and laughing. Some gasped. "Duane Pederson? It must be a joke. He can't do the lead . . ."

"It must be a mistake," someone else said. "He stutters."

When I looked at the board I noticed, to my utter amazement, that I had won the lead. Suddenly I was aware that all the kids were staring at me. A couple of them managed a weak, "Congratulations!" but I gasped out some reply and headed back to the dorm.

My mental anguish was paralyzing. I had hardly said two words in public in my entire life, now I had been saddled with the lead to a college play. The irony of the situation was complete. I had done the whole thing on impulse, to prove to myself— and others, I guess—that I could do it if I wanted to. Now it was in my lap. And I didn't know what to do.

After a sleepless night I said to myself, "I know what I'll do. I'll tell the director that the whole thing was a hoax. Then I'll back out."

But the more I thought about it, the more I felt I had to do it. At least give it a try. I had desperately sought for identity. Now a chance had come my way. From somewhere in the depths of my shattered self concept, I knew I had to do it.

I looked at myself in the mirror. "Duane," I said, "You got yourself into this. Now, you're going to go all the way!"

So I went to rehearsals, and worked hard. We were about two weeks along on the play when the director called me into his office. I thought, "This is it. He's going to let me go . . ."

He said, "Duane, when you tried out for the play I didn't know you stuttered."

By now I really wanted to do the part. But all I could say was, "Yes." And I just sat there numbly, disappointed because I was sure this was the end.

He grinned and stuck out his hand. "But don't worry about it. We're going to work it out . . . you're in!"

"And let me have the part?" I stammered.

"That's right."

I was so relieved, tears welled up in my eyes. I knew the man's reputation as a director, was aware of some of the productions he had put on, and was very grateful for his affirmation. His confidence in me was a tremendous shot in the arm. Coupled with the fact that I had recently discovered and was reading an inspirational book by Dr. Norman Vincent Peale, I began taking several steps forward.

The book emphasized the power of the Scriptures, citing such examples as, "If God be for us, who can be against us?" and, "I can do all things through Christ, who strengtheneth me." These and other verses helped me to begin building my faith in something outside of myself. It was through these two experiences that I began to overcome my problem of stuttering.

Before this I had spent a lot of my time doing sleight-of-hand magic. But with the bolstering of my confidence, I began working professionally. However, I had previously always pantomimed my act. Little by little, though, I began discovering the value of comedy, learned to laugh at myself, and began to make great progress in the field of entertainment.

My world was exciting and I loved it. I didn't know at that time that this glitter was soon to tarnish. But it did.

Several years later, totally disillusioned, and no longer starry-eyed with wonder at the glare of footlights and smell of grease paint, I was working the night club circuit. My little dreams were beginning to disappear. I had long since learned that applause did not provide total satisfaction.

So I tried to retreat from the world of harsh reality through drugs, booze . . . and about everything else. But none of those things did the job I hoped they would. Each escape effort failed. Each "return" to reality found me lonely. I still lived pretty much in a world of fantasy. I was nowhere . . .

I honestly believe that the deep love I have for street people—and all the others that might be called "society rejects"—is because I have experienced everything they have. During my 14 years as an entertainer I was always on the road. And I had no real home either . . .

But all that changed in a night club in Minneapolis. A friend of mine who had been a singer and dancer for the Lawrence Welk Show came into the club. I said, "Let's have lunch together."

"All right," he said. And we set the time and place.

When we got together the next day he began to share Jesus Christ with me. He started back in the Old Testament and talked about David and Jonathan.

"Duane, the love that they shared was the kind of love that far surpassed anything either of them had ever known."

I nodded, taking it all in, my heart growing hungry for something I couldn't quite define. Then he jolted me. "In fact, Duane, Jesus Christ shows the very same love to each of us . . ."

"He does?" I stammered. "Jesus does?"

"That's right." Then he paused for what seemed like a long time.

To break the silence, I said, "Is it for real?"

"Yes, every word of it. You know, my life used to be—all messed up."

"Yes. But, where does this Jesus fit into the picture? He's for the good guys, isn't He?"

My friend chuckled. "Not really. Jesus said, 'I didn't come to call the righteous and all the religious people to repentance. But I came to call sinners.' And, Duane, I was a sinner. No question about that . . ."

Not knowing what else to say, I said, "You're sure right."

He leaned toward me and his eyes bored right into mine. "Duane, that's all over with now. Jesus

Christ has given me something I never had. It's groovy. Neat. I've never felt this way before."

Another pause. My friend drummed his fingers on the table and waited. Almost hesitantly I finally said, "How about me? I need to get hold of the same thing you've got." And to myself I was thinking: *Please let it be for me, too. This is what I want. What I've been wanting for all my life.*

"Sure. All you've got to do is just ask Him to take over your life. And He'll do it."

"When?"

"Right now."

"Right here?"

"Yes, right here."

So I bowed my head. There were people all around, but that didn't matter. In a plain, simple way I said, "Jesus, I'm a sinner. My life's all messed up. I've got no goal. No future. My highs don't satisfy anymore. Please forgive my sins . . . And, how about taking over Duane Pederson's life . . . from right now."

And something happened at that moment.

I felt different, and yet I wasn't different. I didn't know what had happened to me until some time later as I was reading in the Bible, where the Apostle Paul was trying to describe the experience I had just had. He said, "Therefore, If any man be in Christ, he is a new creature. Old things are passed away. Behold, all things are become new" (2 Corinthians 5:17).

I left the club that day.

As I left I said to the manager, "Something great

14

has happened to me. My life is different . . ."

He laughed. "Sure, Duane. You've had a couple. Sure, it's different."

"I mean it. Things are not the same. I'm leaving."

He grinned knowingly. "You'll be back."

I said, "No, I won't." That was several years ago, and I never did go back. I never will. I've got something too great to give up.

Thousands upon thousands of **Free Papers.**

CHAPTER TWO

"Don't Mention My Name!"

In a very real sense, God provided the money for that first issue. And, He has done the same for each one since. I didn't have any money to produce it with. So I prayed again, "Jesus, guide me . . ." Then I set out to share my vision.

I knew a few businessmen in Hollywood, and God seemed to say, "Go to them. Share your vision with them." So I did. The first man I contacted listened patiently, but he kept rearranging the things on his desk while I talked. "How much is it going to cost to produce this . . . this . . . ?"

"Christian underground paper."

"Well, whatever. How much?"

"I'm not sure. Something like five or six hundred dollars."

He whistled. "And how much you got now?"

"Nothing. You're the first man I've contacted."

He looked uncomfortable, but I sat there patiently. He fumbled with his wallet. "Well, here, Duane." He grunted a little embarrassed sound and handed me a folded ten-dollar bill. I stood up and thanked him. As I shook his hand, he didn't quite look me in the eye when he said, "Don't mention my name in the paper. Understand?"

"Yes. I understand. I won't mention it."

"Well, uh . . . good luck, Duane."

I looked him right in the eye again. "God love you."

Suddenly he was very busy looking up something in his desk appointment book. He didn't speak again as I let myself out. I didn't contact him again for help.

And I didn't mention his name in the paper.

The rest of the day was much like this. But I remember one man whom I had befriended a number of times. I had never witnessed to him before. Apparently he had heard what had happened to me. When his secretary announced me, Dave met me at the door, his hand extended. "Duane!" his big voice boomed. "It's good to see you . . . even with the beard." He laughed, and so did I.

"Dave, something beautiful has happened to me," I began.

"Tell me about it."

So I shared Jesus Christ with my old friend. I

simply told him how I had found release from all the old hangups, the old rat-race existence. I told him how Jesus Christ had made me into a new creature. "He's for real, Dave. Jesus Christ is for real . . ."

Dave was looking down at his hands. They were tense. The knuckles were white. Moisture ran down his cheeks unheeded. When he looked up, my old friend said, "Duane, could Jesus Christ do that for me?"

"Yes. He can do it for you. He can forgive your sins, Dave. He can make your life into a thrilling experience."

"He can do all that? You know how I've been living, Duane."

"Yes, I know. Jesus knows that, too. But that doesn't matter. He can change all that. . . . Will you let Him do it?"

He took a deep breath. Just then the phone rang, and as he moved to answer it, the spell was broken. But a trace of the hungry look was still there as he held his hand over the phone. "Duane, tell my secretary to write a check for fifty dollars. This is an important call. Got to take it. And . . . come back. Okay?"

I nodded, gripped his hand, and left. I've seen him since, but he's always been too busy to let God get to him again. Someday, though. Someday another chance will come to introduce him to my Jesus. I'm sure of that.

That evening I thought I had enough money, so I went to a printer with a sketch of what I planned to do. "When can you have all the copy?" he asked.

"Tomorrow morning."

"Tomorrow morning! Man, that's a lot of space to fill."

"I know. But I'll have it."

"When do you need the paper. Printed, I mean?"

"The next morning."

He looked like I'd hit him with something. "You're crazy. It can't be done . . ."

So I simply shared with him my vision as I had to all the others. How I knew that the very best way to communicate thoughts and ideas was through a newspaper. I told him about all those people on the street. "They need Jesus Christ," I said. "I can't talk to all of them. But a paper can."

He looked at his work table, piled high, and kind of shook his head. "Well, I don't know how. But . . ." he looked up and grinned. "Tell your Jesus to help me and I'll do it."

"I'll tell Him. And He will help you."

I already had in mind what to call it—The *Hollywood Free Paper*—and what would go into that first issue. And I went home that night and put it together. It was a very simple paper. In fact all of them are. On the front page I used part of the dialogue between Art Linkletter and his daughter that they recorded just six weeks before she was murdered by those who manufacture and sell drugs.

There was a page of Scripture, in bold, hand printing that proclaimed from the Book of Hebrews: "The man who approaches God must have faith in two things, first that God exists and secondly that it is worth a man's while to try and find God" (Hebrews 11:6).

Then, in a simple editorial, I "launched" the *Hollywood Free Paper*. Briefly, this is what I said:

"Hollywood Free Paper supports and seeks to propagate the teachings of Jesus Christ. The only reason we do this is because we have already tried almost every means to reach God that man has thought of and at the end of this search turned to the One who said 'I am the way, the truth, and the life.' He also said 'I am come that they might have life, and that they might have it more abundantly.' (A full, complete and exciting life.)

"When you come to the time in your life that you have tried everything else and want to really start living on an eternal high, but you're not really sure if God is for real and that He loves you and wants for you to discover that love . . . Just try this—Say . . . 'God, I don't know where You are, but if You *are* and can hear me right now . . . even though I'm not sure what it is all about . . . if Jesus was right and is the way to knowing You, I invite You to make Yourself real to me. I make no promises, but I do want to experience Your Spirit. I need you!'

"That's it. The rest is up to God. 'Too simple,' you say . . . Well, if you want that to be your hang-up . . . that's your hang-up. All we can do is tell you we've experienced it. It has changed our lives.

"INTERESTED? WRITE: FREE PAPER, BOX 1949, HOLLYWOOD, CALIF. 90028."

I was kind of bleary-eyed, but very excited when I delivered my night's work to the printer early the next morning. He was surprised when I walked in. "I didn't think you'd make it. But I was sort of hoping you would."

"Well, you told me to ask my Jesus for help. So I did."

He grunted. "Okay, how many copies you want?"

"Ten thousand."

"*Ten thousand*?"

"That's right. How much will that be?"

He figured for a couple of minutes and quoted a figure. "I don't have that amount yet," I told him. "But I'll have it when you have the job finished." And I did. God helped me do it.

He delivered right on time.

Then I went out on the street with bundles of *Free Papers* and I handed them out to everybody who passed by. It didn't take as long as I thought. And I was almost sorry when they were gone. I prayed as I gave them out, "Oh, Jesus, this brother is strung out on about everything. Reach through all that haze and change his life."

And, "Dear God, this sister is selling herself every day, over and over. Eternity is written on her face. An eternity of suffering. Please let her see that Jesus Christ is the answer . . . her answer."

Very few people refused to take the paper. And nobody dropped them on the sidewalk. It thrilled me to see little knots of street people standing and reading the paper God had helped me—more than that—*the paper God had compelled me to publish.*

SATAN'S SNOWSTORM: BIGGEST SNOW JOB IN HISTORY!

CHAPTER THREE

The Letters Come In

I didn't think very many people would be affect-
ed by the simple message of the Gospel, and I was
a little let down when the last one was gone. I was
very tired, but knew I couldn't sleep. So I went to
a nearby coffee house for my cup of hot tea. I was
praying all the time for those who received a copy
of the paper . . .

All the time I was distributing the *Free Paper* I
was wondering if anybody would really read it, and
I was almost sure that they wouldn't. Then I won-
dered if I'd hear from anybody, and I was almost
sure that I wouldn't hear a word.

But a couple of days later my mailbox was jammed with mail from people, mostly street people, who wanted to know more about the Jesus Christ we were talking about in the paper! Praise the Lord!

Many of the letters were written in pencil. Many were scrawled on scraps of paper, barely legible, poorly spelled. A few were typewritten. But all of them expressed the same hunger:

"If your Jesus Christ is really for real, man, I
want to know more. I'd like to rap with you
about the guy. Where can we meet? When?
Are you gonna have another paper?"

The response was thrilling. But it was a little bit frightening, too. How could I answer all the letters? Some of them didn't even have addresses. Some were signed with just a first name. A few gave a telephone number. Some sent in dollar bills for their "subscription" to the *Free Paper*. All at once the realization came to me that I was committed to publish another edition. And another. I could sense God leading me. Even giving me a little shove now and then.

I remember talking to God about all this. "Dear God, this is all more than I expected. But if You want me to keep on printing the paper I'll do it. But You've certainly got to keep on helping me to do it. I believe this is where it's at, Jesus. So, as long as You keep leading me . . . and keep on providing the means . . . well, then I'll just keep on telling everybody I can about what You can do if You're given a chance."

Some of the people who had helped me with the first paper decided they "couldn't afford" to help with the next one. Especially when they saw the first one. One man met me at his door when his secretary told him I was there. He said, "Sorry, Duane. That's it. I think the paper's pretty bad, and I can't support it."

Another man who had been my friend for years said, "Nobody can change these street freaks. You're wasting your time. If you want to preach, get a church or something. These bums on the street don't appreciate what you're trying to do . . ."

"Look," I said, "these freaks and bums, as you put it, are people . . ."

"No they're not!" he interrupted. "They're drop outs. Runaways. They're no good or they wouldn't have left home in the first place. Now they're messing up the boulevard. Everywhere you go you see them! They stink. I want to get them out of here. And you're just encouraging them to stay."

I tried to tell him that Jesus Christ loved them, and that He was their only hope. But he wouldn't listen.

But there was one man who has been in this thing up to his neck from the start. His name is Lawrence Young, a tremendous man. In his sixties, I think. But he's right in there. To see him put his arm around a barefoot, levi-clad long-hair and hear him tell them that Jesus loves them, is a heartening sight. It makes me realize that God can reach people through people. It makes me grateful over and over again that there doesn't have to be a so-called "generation gap" or "communications breakdown."

Lawrence has always been right there when I needed him with an encouraging word or some constructive criticism or help. He's a businessman in Hollywood, but he's also the head of counselling at our Jesus Festivals.

One man who helped financially a time or two got mad when I mentioned his name in the paper, and he's never given anything since. "I don't want to be associated with such a paper. Or with such a movement," he said. "Just keep my name out of it. Sorry about that. But that's the way it is."

I was working again as an entertainer, so for the next two or three issues I put my own money into printing the paper. The first issue was 10,000. The second was 15,000. The third was 20,000. Then we jumped to 35,000.

But for our next issue—New Year's Day—we did something that was almost beyond our scope. We went all out and printed 100,000 copies. We went over to Pasadena and dropped them at the Civic Auditorium where there was a Gospel rock concert going on.

In the middle of the concert one of the guys shared with the audience that there were plenty of *Free Papers* outside, and that they were there to hand out on Colorado Boulevard that night. If you've ever been to the Rose Parade, you know it begins to happen the day before. About noon on the last day of December, the streets are already lined with people. They come with their sleeping bags, their thermos jugs of coffee. Some of them even bring charcoal grills and cook their meals right on the street.

So this was a natural way to hand out the papers. To my absolute amazement, the people from the audience came out and took all the papers that were there. There seemed to be some sort of drawing, magnetic force about them. The people wanted to touch a copy, to read it. Because at that time the paper was still pretty far out for most people. They had heard of the *Free Paper*. Some of them had even read one before. But here they were, thousands of them. And they went wild. Of course, some of the Christian people were not willing to accept a copy, and not even able to accept the fact that it was a legitimate media for getting Christ to the street people. This has changed to some degree since then.

The impact of the paper on that crowd of over a million people staggered me. Of course, the papers didn't get to all the crowd. They only got a little way up and down Colorado Blvd., but not to the far ends. But from the outreach of that one issue I got over 600 letters from people who read the paper and prayed and invited Jesus Christ into their lives.

During that one night over 600 people—that we know about—accepted Jesus Christ, as a result of the *Free Paper!* All we could say was, "Praise the Lord!" "Praise the Lord!"

This next year, New Year's Day, we planned ahead. I went to the police department. "How many people do you expect along the Parade route?" I asked them.

They had it all figured out. "We expect about one million, six hundred thousand," they told me.

So we started figuring. We checked the statistics for newspaper readership of a tabloid such as ours, and learned that an average of eight people read each copy. That meant that if I would print 200,000 copies of the paper, and find a means of distributing them throughout the entire crowd, that there was the potential means of contacting every single person in that immense crowd with the message of Jesus Christ!

And so we did it — we printed 200,000!

Someone said, "Duane, you're crazy! It won't work! You'll go broke. And it won't be that much more effective."

"I know it sounds crazy," I said. "But I believe that's what God wants us to do. I believe He's going to supply the money to print that many papers. And to help us distribute them. And if He's going to help us, we don't dare not do it."

And God worked out the details so beautifully. He always does when we trust Him.

So we had the papers available at a rock concert the Sunday prior to New Year's Eve. We called it the First Annual Jesus People Festival of Music. It was the first one we'd ever had so it had to be the "first."

And the responses we got back! We're still getting letters from people who read that issue, five or six months afterward. Close to 2,000 people who read the paper, accepted Jesus Christ into their lives as a result of that one single effort. Once again we say, "Praise the Lord!"

Somehow, God has helped us to move ahead with every issue. This current issue is 350,000. Much of this is now being printed outside of Southern California. *I now have the vision, with God's help, to print over 1,000,000 copies.* All of this to the glory of Jesus Christ.

It's so rewarding . . . exciting, is a better word . . . to realize that through the printed page, the *Hollywood Free Paper,* that lonely, hungry, hung-up, spaced out, sick-of-it-all people are finding Jesus Christ as the Answer. And He is the only answer to the desperate needs of the human heart.

The paper goes to each of the 50 states now, and nearly a dozen foreign countries. Every day we get letters from people all over—who want to re-print the paper and distribute it right where they are. And, of course, we give them permission.

A lot of people wonder what the *Hollywood Free Paper* is all about. If you'd like a sample copy, just write to: HOLLYWOOD FREE PAPER, BOX 1949, Hollywood, Calif. 90028, and we'll send you one. But the following lead article in one of the early issues will give you a good idea of the whole reason for the paper's existence:

CAN YOU DIG IT?

By

Rich Schmidt

I know you can dig that almost everyone today is hung-up. Why? Because you have been sold a phony bill of goods concerning reality. You have let the "system" pull the wool over your eyes regarding who Jesus Christ really is. I don't blame you for getting up-tight with the Christianity that most churches peddle. You get the idea that Jesus is some kind of a prejudiced, middle-class materialist or else some kind of a milk-toast character that wants to spoil your bag with a bunch of rules and regulations. But, Jesus promises you life and liberty. He said, "I have come to give you a real meaningful and abundant life."

Jesus Christ is no namby-pamby character. In fact, Christ really socks it to you with some real heavy stuff. He said, "I have come as light into the world, that everyone who puts their trust in Me may not remain in darkness" (John 12:46). Jesus wants to give you light on what's really happening.

Jesus said, "If you can dig on the words I have spoken to you, then you are really My disciples; you will know the truth and the truth will set you free" (John 8:31-32). The truth is, that Jesus Christ is the Way, the Truth, and the Life. Without the Way there is no going; without the Truth there is no knowing; and without the Life there is no living.

Jesus Christ is truly the Cool One because He took the rap for you and me on the cross, so that we could have life—the real down-inside kind of life that hits at the very core of your being. Even though we have all blown it, Christ died for us. Some have messed up more than others, but we're all in the same boat when it comes to being a sinner. The good news is that God is willing to pardon us if we're willing to admit we're sinners in need of a Savior. I know this bothers a lot of people because it's unsophisticated and unfashionable to say you

are a sinner. But remember this: "It was after the world in its wisdom had failed to find God, that He in His wisdom chose to save those who would believe in the simple, unsophisticated message of the gospel."

Do you want freedom from being hung-up? To be truly free you must thank God that Jesus took the rap for your sins and put your faith in Him. For Christ said, "Truly, truly, I say to you, everyone who commits sin is the slave of sin . . . But, if the Son of God sets you free, you will be free indeed!"

Check it out and see if the things Christ said and did don't jive with reality. I mean, a guy who said the things Jesus said would either have to be the Son of God or some kind of nut.

Being a follower of Christ is truly where it's at. It's a groovy program, but it's not an easy one. In fact, it's so heavy that Jesus said, "You had better count the cost and see if you have what it takes to be my disciple." Following Christ doesn't mean having your own bag and doing your own thing.

Instead of getting up-tight with the "system," get hep to what the Bible says about Jesus Christ and about you and not what a lot of hung-up people try to tell you. If your bag is Jesus Christ, it's a heavenly trip all the way. But, if Christ is not your bag then it's bad news for you because you're on an eternal bummer.

Jesus Christ busted out of the grave nearly 2,000 years ago; right now, He wants to bust into your life and make you aware of His program.

CHAPTER FOUR

Jesus People: For Real?

Everywhere I go people ask, "Who are these Jesus People? Are they for real?"

"Is it a new denomination?"

"What's it all about?"

"How did you get involved in it?"

"What do Jesus People believe in?"

Well, to begin with, no person started the Jesus People Movement. God did that. I coined the name after I launched the *Free Paper,* but I didn't start the Movement. It was spontaneous, clearly led by the Holy Spirit. The Movement started several places at the same time: in Seattle. San Francisco. Los Angeles. And others . . .

Originally the press called us Jesus Freaks. On the street and within the Jesus Movement, the word "freak" isn't a bad word. A freak is someone who has gone to an extreme on anything—even Jesus Christ.

On the street, the word described the people who were dropping too much acid, or "speed"—or so much of something that they "freaked out." So they were called "acid freaks" or "speed freaks"— or some other kind of "freak," depending what they were "freaked out" on.

Basically it was speed, because that would really freak them out even more than acid. Acid is more of a head trip. But speed does something complete, something totally destructive to the person. A guy who's been a speed freak for a while gets "spaced out." His mind, or part of it, gets wiped out, destroyed.

One day as I was talking to one of the newsmen he said, "Those street people who get turned on for Jesus are freaks—'Jesus Freaks.'"

I said, "They're not freaks. They're people. They're Jesus People." Somehow the name stuck, and now the movement is called the Jesus People Movement.

It started as a ministry to the street people—the thousands upon thousands of people who live on the streets. These people exist in abandoned buildings, on roof tops, in alleys, parks, on the beaches. And many of them live in VW busses. They have no other homes than the street.

According to the authorities over a million kids a

year leave home and wander to Hollywood. They aren't just Californians. They are boys and girls from the farm in Iowa or Texas. From the house next door. They aren't always from the "down-and-out" neighborhood. Far from it. They are the neighbors to everybody in America.

Most of the street people are called drop-outs or runaways. But they are people. Real people. They may not matter to their own community or family. But they matter to Jesus Christ. They matter to Him very much. He came to seek and to save them.

Though the Movement started as a ministry to the street people, it is much wider than that now. It is reaching the campuses—both high school and college. And it's definitely ministering to the youth of the establishment churches.

God has given me a feeling of great urgency about ministering to these people. It's extremely difficult to put that feeling into words. I can't describe it. I wish I could. It's a certain drive I have to touch and to love somebody who is unloved—and sometimes unlovely. Somebody who may not have had a bath in many, many weeks—because of being on the road and sleeping on the street.

Someone made the remark that, "All today's kids need is a sleeping bag and a thumb and they can go anywhere."

That's quite literally true. They can go anywhere, but they still have no place to sleep or to take a bath.

This compelling force I have for the street people is one that no human force has created. It is not an emotion. It is a love which the Holy Spirit gives. It compels you to love everybody . . .

I think this love I have for the street people somewhat illustrates the love that Christ expressed toward the woman who was thrown at His feet by some church leaders.

"Master," they said, "this woman should be stoned to death. She was caught in the very act of adultery."

Jesus didn't say anything.

He merely bent down, and in a casual, easy way He wrote in the sand. After a while He looked up and said to the religious folks who were standing around, "Whoever among you has no sin, let him cast the first stone."

Then Jesus bent down and wrote in the sand again. One by one the woman's accusers guiltily crept away. When He looked up again she was alone.

"Where are your accusers?"

"They are all gone, Lord."

"I don't accuse you. Go and sin no more."

Revolutionary Jesus forgave that woman. He showed love to her. How revolutionary to show love! When the people standing on the outside—hating her, ready, with stones in hand, to treat her to a violent death—showed no love. Jesus' attitude was revolutionary—one of understanding. One of love.

The Jesus People Movement is a movement of love. It isn't a new denomination. It isn't even a church. It's a movement, made up of people who

Sharing the Word of God.

Larry Norman, popular Jesus People singer/composer/
writer.

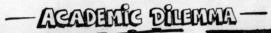

express love when they come face to face with lonely, frightened, completely lost people.

The street people—for one reason or another—are castoffs from society. But the love that Jesus gives me for them causes them to respond. And as a result, many of them come to Jesus Christ. The Jesus People exemplify Jesus' love. Simply. Beautifully, without undue display.

They believe in Jesus Christ as Savior and Lord. He is the cornerstone of our faith. We believe in Jesus, and in His power to save, to change lives. The Jesus People "doctrine" is simply: "Jesus Christ is the only way . . ."

CHAPTER FIVE

"Christ Is Where It's At . . ."

Since that day in Minneapolis when I met Jesus
Christ—when He became a living force in my life—
I have shared Him wherever I go.

I pick up hitchhikers.

And each time I do I try to reach out to them.
I don't always share Jesus Christ with them in words,
but in action.

The reason I do this is two-fold. Christ took away
my loneliness and fear. I know that these street
people are full of both, and I want to let them know
they can have freedom from fear. That it can be
turned into peace.

Often I greet my passengers with, "God loves you, friend."

To some this is startling and it opens the door to a further sharing of Christ. To others it is a warm, friendly greeting that they respond to, making it even easier to reach out to them.

The second reason that I feel such an urgency to touch these people is that life is so fleeting. In a literal sense we pass like ships in the night, and there is so little time to do all that must be done.

We might be in the car only ten or fifteen miles. I know that when they get in with me that I will have only a few minutes to share Christ with them, then they'll be gone. And I might never see them again.

That's so much what life is all about. Christ described it as a blade of grass that sprouts up quickly. Then the sun comes along and it withers. It dries up. The wind comes and it is blown away, and is no more. So every chance I get, I share Jesus Christ. For I know I may never see that person again. And I usually don't. We touch briefly. I put on the brakes. He opens the door, says "Take care," and is gone.

I pray as the light changes and I drive away, "Jesus, let the power of Your name reach into his heart . . ."

I know that I possess something in my heart that the street people need . . . that they are hungry for. And I am compelled to tell them about it.

Unless you've been involved in the street movement you cannot possibly know what it really is.

It's a counter-culture that doesn't come to the surface unless you've been around on the streets for quite a while. It's different than anything else, than any other culture.

For one thing, there's a very "together" feeling among the people on the street. They take everybody to be their brother and sister—in the truest sense of the word. Everybody they come in contact with they're willing to take in, to share everything they might have.

For example, if you go around hitchhiking, and you happen to have long hair, and if you're alone, it's not unusual for a funky old VW bus that's all painted up to stop and pick you up. Then, as soon as you get going, they open up a little door behind the seat, and pull out all sorts of health foods, and perhaps some cheese and a bottle of wine.

As you're going along, they insist you eat—and give you whatever they have. This is a great underlying feeling and force within the whole street culture—this totally unselfish willingness to share whatever they have.

After you've eaten all you can hold, and drunk all you want, they might haul out the stash and give you some pot. So you can get high as well as drunk and full. And when you're in that condition, all of a sudden they say, "Oh, this is where we turn off."

Then you get out of the car at three or so in the morning, stoned, drunk and sick—in the middle of nowhere.

It's not that they meant to just "drop you off" there. But it's as simple as this: that was where they had to turn off. And it's almost a parody to the street existence—that all of a sudden the beautiful "togetherness" you had a few minutes before is gone, and you are in a far worse condition than you were to begin with.

I think that's a pretty accurate picture of the street existence. For a while you are alone. Then you are with someone for a time. *Then you are alone again.* Very much alone.

But that very fact is part of the key of the Jesus People Movement. The street people share everything they have with everybody! They don't apologize for what they have. They just say, "Here, have some. Have some cheese. Or have some bread . . ." Or whatever.

And the same thing happens when they meet Jesus Christ. When they meet you they very naturally say, "I want you to meet Jesus Christ. He's where it's at. He'll give you the peace you're after."

These street Christians—the Jesus People—do this without any hesitation. It's a matter of sharing something else they have. This time it's their new-found Friend. They feel compelled to do this. That's the way they live. It's beautiful.

They take Christ's words seriously where He says, "Go. And tell . . ."

Because of this natural "outgoingness" the Jesus People Movement is spreading like wildfire. That's why it is blossoming and multiplying like it is. And it will continue to spread as long as people remain open and loving as they are now.

So you see, Jesus People aren't freaks. They're

people. Real, live people. People for whom Jesus died. I wish people on the "outside" could remember that.

Numberless times people ask me, "Are they for real? Are the Jesus People serious? Or is this all a passing fad?"

My answer is, "Praise God! Of course they're real. This is not a fad. It's a true, spontaneous movement of the Holy Spirit. The Prophet Joel spoke of this in the Old Testament. He said, 'And it shall come to pass afterward, that I will pour out my spirit upon all flesh; and your sons and daughters *(these are the street people)* shall prophesy, your old men shall dream dreams, your young men shall see visions:

" 'And also upon the servants and upon the handmaids in those days *(that's today)* will I pour out my spirit!' (Joel 2:28, 29).

"Maybe some of them are like the seed Jesus tells falls on stony ground, and they have no depth, and wither away. But most of them are genuine examples of the grace of God."

What more can we ask? God performs the miracles in our lives. It's up to us to let Him do that. He does perform those miracles in the lives of the street people. Even as He does in the lives of the "straights" . . . *but maybe more so.*

Why? Because these people have gotten down to basics. They are facing life's realities. The nitty gritty. And when Jesus Christ says, "Come unto me . . ." they do. And when He says, "Go!" they go. They love and serve Him openly, without pretense.

Jesus Christ is willing to make real, honest-to-goodness people . . . Christ-like people . . . out of all of us.

"The Word of God is quick and powerful . . ."

CHAPTER SIX

Controversy!

After I found Jesus Christ back there in Minneapolis I became involved in a large church there. I joined a choir, was invited to be on a telecast. And I was part of it all. It was the first time, really, that I felt like I was a vital part of anything. It felt good. The pastor believed that you "Use them or lose them!" So he did his best to use me.

I began studying the Word of God, and it was there that the Bible came alive for me. I thank God for those days.

Invitations began coming to speak for and entertain at youth rallies. Before long I was full-time— and was on the road constantly.

Then the opportunity came for me to go to a Bible college in the Midwest. And it was there, through much pain and controversy that *God began to shape my life for work among the street people.*

I was a typical Northern boy and stumbled into some situations I didn't know how to handle. One of them was mixed bathing.

When I had grown up in Minnesota I had never worried much about swimming. When it got hot, I would just cut across the tracks and take a dip in the lake next to our farm. All the kids did it, both boys and girls. We had a great time. Now I suddenly discovered that things were not quite that simple anymore . . .

I first learned this one hot, muggy Friday afternoon. What could be better and nicer, I reasoned, than to go for a swim on a day like today? So I went to the city pool and had a very refreshing swim. I learned of the error of my ways that evening at the college cafeteria.

I was sitting at the table with some of the more pious students. I noticed them giving me side glances, but thought nothing of it. That is, till they began making comments.

"Hot day, Duane," one of the fellows said.

"Hot? It's horrible!" I answered.

"Your hair's all wet. You must really sweat in this weather."

I walked into their trap. "Yeah, I sweat a lot on days like this. But I got my head wet swimming."

The smug nods went around the table.

"Swimming? Hmmm . . . Where did you go? Out

at the river?"

"No. Over at the city pool."

"City pool. Is that right?"

"You mean to say, Duane . . ." the leader said, "that you went swimming today? Mixed bathing?"

My caustic strain got the best of me for a moment. "Mixed bathing? I didn't see any black people there."

A gasp went around the table. When my opponent recovered, he said, "Not black and white. Boys and girls."

That was the beginning of things to come. I didn't quit my afternoon swimming, but the group quit me. I was practically ostracized by virtually everyone who was there for the summer.

When the fall semester started I talked to one of the pastors of a large church about serving some way. He looked embarrassed but didn't answer right away. I thought he might not have heard me, so I repeated my question.

"Pastor, I've served as a youth evangelist and I've done some Bible teaching. Now, while I'm in college, I'd like to help out in church . . ."

He cleared his throat. "Well, Duane . . . m-m-m . . . uh, as much as I'd like to, I don't think I can."

I was dumbfounded. "What do you mean, you can't use me? I know you need Sunday school teachers, and others."

"Well, you see, there's been some talk about . . ." And he went on to tell me that because I was an entertainer—"and it's such an evil profession . . . —we'd like to sort of observe you for a while before we could, uhh . . . entrust you with any responsibilities here at the church."

A fist in the gut could not have hurt me more. But, more than being hurt, I was deeply wounded. It took me back years ago when I had been refused "admittance to the circle" because of my stuttering, my inability to communicate. But this was even worse, I thought. Now I was qualified (I honestly believed) to serve Jesus Christ—and the church was withholding their permission. It didn't seem to make sense. It still doesn't.

As a child I had retreated into a fantasy life when I was rejected. Now things were different. I felt a compulsion to serve the Lord—somehow, some way.

So I opened up a teen club in Springfield and called it Funland. It started out to be an indoor miniature golf course. But that didn't work out too well, so I added a juke box, some pinball machines and some pool tables, and turned it into an amusement center.

This didn't go over too well at the college and they tried to close me up. But since one of the professors had a pool table in his own house, they didn't say too much. But it was during this time that relations with the college deteriorated quite badly. Because of the attitude of some of the students and professors, I began to lose interest. Consequently my grades took a nose-dive. But I didn't care. Satan had begun to work in my life and I found it much easier to cheat on exams than to study. So I did.

Of course I got caught.

One day I was called into the Dean's office.

When I walked in I found myself facing the entire administrative council (I called them the Sanhedrin). The Dean held up some papers and asked, "Are these yours?"

I looked at them. "Yes, Sir. They are mine."

"We have reason to believe that you have been cheating. Since this is a very serious offense, please be careful how you answer."

He paused to let this sink in. "Have you, Mr. Pederson, been cheating?"

I couldn't see any sense lying about it. So I answered quickly, "Yes, sir, I have."

They asked me how I had gone about it, and I told them. They asked me to apologize to the committee and I did. They told me they knew others were involved and asked me to name then, even though they already knew who they were. I refused. When they called the others on the carpet, they denied any knowledge of the charge, and refused to apologize for something "they knew nothing about."

I was dismissed from the college, while the others remained. I couldn't see that justice had been done and left the college with feelings of bitterness.

Meanwhile the club was doing very well. I started having rock bands come in and began charging admission. Crowds began to flock to the club and I began to do quite well financially. Though I still didn't feel good about the college, I had confessed my wrongs and received forgiveness. Then the Lord began using me again in a rather unusual way.

People began coming to me with some serious questions like: "Duane, what's life all about anyway?"

And, "I'm all messed up. What am I going to do?"

"I'm getting freaked out on speed. I can't stop. I'm scared!"

I shared Jesus Christ with them. It seemed that about every evening I would spend time talking to the people one by one about turning on to Jesus. It was thrilling to be able to talk to the kids who were so hungry and to point them to Jesus Christ.

I began to sense God's leading again. And *over a period of six weeks over 100 people found Jesus Christ when I witnessed to them!* Dimly I began to see a purpose in it all.

But not everybody was happy about the situation. Some of the professors and ministers visited me. "Why don't you come back?" they would ask. "Don't keep up this foolishness. There's a petition being circulated to close you up . . ."

I laughed. "Why should I go back? After what you did . . ."

"Because we want you to come back to Christ. We want you to be a Christian."

My bitterness and cynicism came through. "What is a Christian, anyway?" I asked.

They looked at each other and one of them said, "Well . . . a Christian is one who is Christlike." He waved his arm around, indicated the club we were in. "It's not being involved in surroundings like this. With people like this . . ."

That did it. "In reading the Bible I learned that Christ was accused by the religious folk of hanging around with prostitutes and drunkards . . . and all that sort of people. And that's what I'm hanging around with here. So if that's the case I guess that makes me more Christlike than you in your ivory tower." I laid it on.

Then I told them about the ones I had led to the Lord.

They answered, "Then why aren't they in church? What church are they going to?"

I pointed at a young girl wearing black leotards and a black leather jacket who was a member of one of the bike clubs who hung out at the club. "That girl prayed with me just last night and invited Christ into her life."

They didn't look impressed. I said, "Why don't you invite her to Sunday school?"

One of the men answered, "No. We don't want that kind."

I said, "Well, that's your answer. That's why they aren't in any church. And that's why God has me here, in the middle of all this . . . in order that I can introduce them to Christ, then share Christ's life with them in a greater way."

The conclusion of the whole matter was that they got up a petition, signed by the people from the church I was a member of, and by the college I had attended. Over 2,000 people signed it and they took it to my landlord who was a state senator up for re-election within a few weeks. I was given ten days to close the club. Since I had no money to fight it, I had nothing else to do but to close.

During those last few days, though, the club was jammed. One time there were over 350 inside and nearly as many standing outside. Naturally this gave me a great deal of newspaper publicity.

One of the regular attendants of the club was quoted as saying, "Well they're going to close the only place we can go to and relax. I know it usually ends up with Duane Pederson 'preaching to us' but it's a cool place."

Another said, "Now we can go back to throwing rocks at cars. That's about the only thing there's left to do . . ."

I was sorry to leave the Midwest, but I know God knew what He was doing, because He had an even greater work lined up for me.

CHAPTER SEVEN

Rejects Reclaimed

Nobody who actually sees lives changed through the power of Jesus Christ can doubt the power of the Gospel. It may not be understood, or even fully "agreed" with, but it cannot be denied. At our first festival I saw this happen to Jim. He was fifteen, was dressed in levis and sandals.

I saw him during the meeting, more than that, I was drawn to him. The music got to him. So did the simple message I gave. Nothing elaborate. Just that Jesus Christ came into this world to reach those who felt nobody cared. And that Jesus loved everybody. Jim came to me that evening and said, "Did you mean what you said tonight, Duane?"

"What do you mean?"

"That part about this Jesus loving . . . you know . . . loving everybody. I mean, no matter what they'd done?"

"Yes, Jim. I meant it."

"Are you sure about that. I mean . . . does He even love me?"

"Yes, Jim. Jesus loves you. He loves you very much."

"No matter what I've done?"

"Jim, it doesn't make any difference what you might have done—what anybody's done. Or what they haven't done. Jesus Christ came into the world to forgive us our sins, and to redeem us."

Jim was silent. He was very serious. His long hair framed a face that looked too young to be totally on its own. He finally took a deep breath. "Okay, Duane, I believe you."

Very softly I said, "And do you receive Him . . .?"

He nodded. "Yes, I want Him to come into my life."

We prayed, Jim and I, and the boy simply invited Christ into his life. He didn't show great emotion, didn't even shed tears, if I remember right. But his life was clearly changed.

A few days later he came and asked to talk to me.

Though Jim still had a look of peace about him, I could tell he was troubled about something.

"I've got some things I've got to tell you," he began.

"Okay."

"Well, I'm from Iowa. A small town out in the sticks. I did a lot of things I'm not proud of. Got into a lot of trouble." He looked up for me to speak, but I just nodded.

He took a deep breath. "I stole some things. Just little things . . . then . . . the motorcycle. I stole it, too. Wanted to get away from home. Things were pretty bad there. So one day I stuffed some things . . . some clothes and things . . . into a bag. I got my sleeping bag. Then I grabbed the bike and left home. Just split. Left the old man a note and headed for California."

"Have you written them?" I asked.

He nodded. "Yeah. Last night. I told them about what happened to me. You know. About Jesus Christ coming into my life. Told them something else, Duane . . ." He hesitated and searched my face with his transparent, gentle smile. I thought I knew what was coming. And I was right.

"Duane, I told them I'm coming home. Going to turn myself in . . . I . . . think that's what Jesus wants me to do. You know, make things right. Like you were telling us about that guy Levi, the tax collector. How he took care of his crimes and stuff when he began to follow Jesus. Right?"

"That's right, Jim. I'm sure Jesus wants you to clean up your life as much as possible . . ."

It was very difficult for me to see that boy—he was only 15—roll up his sleeping-bag and extra pair of levis and start out, the long, long way back. But I thanked God for the power of Jesus Christ that could do something so beautiful in the life of a boy who had turned to Him. So far I've not heard from Jim again. But I think I will some day.

A few weeks ago a friend of mine and I were down at Juvenile Hall where I was speaking in chapel. As we walked by the lineup, one of the boys yelled at us and waved.

My friend waved back. "It's Scot," he said. And I waved too. I vaguely recognized the boy, but my friend knew him.

"Scot accepted Christ at a Bible rap session a week ago," my friend said. "He'd been pretty messed up. Had a pretty rough past. But Christ really changed him."

"Then what's he doing here?" I asked.

"Turned himself in. He told me the L.A. police wanted him for several things. And he said he was going to make things right. It took a lot of guts to do it."

Things like this happen nearly every day—people accepting Jesus Christ, then facing reality, facing life as it really is, then shouldering their responsibilities . . . some of them for the first time in their life. Examples of the power of Jesus Christ. They feel a compelling urge to make their lives right again after Christ has forgiven them and accepted them.

Jack came to our house one afternoon out of nowhere. He'd been down to the Free Clinic getting a tooth pulled. At the Clinic he met this girl and they began to talk. He told her he'd just gotten into town the day before and he had no place to crash. She suggested he come to our house. So, suddenly, there he was. He looked pretty miserable because of the tooth extraction.

When he came in and looked around he said, "Uhhh, I was thinking . . . I mean, can I sleep here tonight? I don't have any place to go. Don't have a bedroll or anything . . ."

We really don't have facilities for anyone to live at the house which is our office, but there always seems to be two or three sleeping there on the floor. But Jack was pretty miserable, just having a tooth pulled, besides being lonely. So I said, "Sure, you can stay here tonight, if you don't mind sleeping on the floor."

"No, I don't mind at all. Beats sleeping in some alley."

The next morning I explained our policy to him. "Jack," I said, "we live by the Bible here. And the Bible makes it clear that if a man doesn't work he doesn't deserve to eat. How does that sound to you?"

"Man, I don't mind working. Not a bit."

"Well, we've got some painting to do around here. Things like that. After you eat, we'll get started."

So Jack stayed that day and did a good job painting. I invited him to stay that night, which he did. This went on for several days. One day after our regular time of prayer and Bible study we were talking, and he began to open up.

"You know, I came across the country with some friends . . . all the way from Georgia. And all the time we were looking for a farm where we could raise the vegetables we needed . . . and, you know, sort of commune with nature."

He looked serious. "But all that time I think what we were really looking for was . . . Jesus."

A day or so later during a prayer time Jack prayed out loud for the first time in his life. He just said, "Jesus, forgive me of my sins. And come into my life."

This man was so gentle before he received Christ, but afterwards there flowed through him such love that it's hard to describe. He was a reject that Christ had reclaimed.

But we don't win them all. It breaks my heart, but it's true. Tom was just such a man. When he came by the center and I told him about Jesus Christ, he immediately accepted Him. A couple of days later he met a girl friend and they started living together. But still they came by for Bible study. They told me they were reading and praying together at home.

Then before I knew it I realized one day when they came in that they were both up on something. I asked him about it.

"Yes, we've been sniffing cocaine."

"Both of you?"

"Yes." As he shifted his eyes around the room.

Soon after that she was back working as a nude dancer in one of the bars. Yet they would come by, but not nearly as often. Then he told me one day that he was reincarnated as J.F.K. Later he said he was Adolf Hitler. Then suddenly they didn't come any more.

I was heartbroken.

But Jesus told us that when we plant the seed some will fall on good ground. Some will fall on stony ground. And some will fall on the path or the street where the birds pick it up. He said that some of the seed would also fall among the thorns.

So when some of the seed falls in infertile places . . . like when someone hears, accepts, and then drifts away . . . I am disappointed, but not discouraged. Because it only proves that the Scriptures are true—that not everyone would become followers of the Master.

I would like for them to, and the Bible says that Jesus didn't want any to perish, but that not all would accept. Jesus, in fact, wept over the city, "O Jerusalem, Jerusalem, thou that killest the prophets, and stonest them which are sent unto thee, how often would I have gathered thy children together, even as a hen gathereth her chickens under her wings, and ye would not!" (Matthew 23:37).

Yet it is so beautiful, when someone comes to Christ, his life is changed, and God's blessings are evident. I wish it could be so with all who have been confronted with Jesus Christ.

Just a few days ago a young couple came to the center. They appeared so happy. So I asked them to tell me what made them so. He was 21 and she 19. They smiled at each other, then he turned to me. "Duane, it's very simple. We found Jesus Christ."

"How did it happen?"

"One of the brothers just told us about Him. How He loves us. And it was such a great story . . . well, we just wanted to know Him. And so . . . we just invited Him to come in."

"And He did," she said.

They held each other's hand. Their smiles were radiant. "Now that we have Jesus . . . we would like you to marry us," he said.

I grasped their hands. "Of course." And we prayed together. It was a thrilling moment.

A few days later I married them in a plain, simple ceremony at the beach. Then I baptized them in the ocean. Their childlike love for each other was beautiful. It was a tremendous day.

CHAPTER EIGHT

Revolutionaries!

As soon as I left the Midwest I headed for California. I was determined not to cooperate with Christians again. It seemed that each time I had done it I got stomped on. I did some work with some youth organizations, but turned down many of their invitations . . .

I had the feeling then that anything I would do must be done alone, because I had gone through too many broken confidences by too many who professed to serve the Lord.

I became a gypsy again.

This went on for some time: school assemblies

and other engagements—all of which kept me on the road all the time. My contacts with people were brief as I was in a different town every day.

But during these months I was praying, "Lord, please use me. I don't know how You are working. I don't know what Your plans are. But, Lord, I am Yours."

Often, in the wee hours of the morning as I lay awake praying I would speak to Him as though He were in the room. "Lord, it seems that I have been turned down by every group I've ever tried to be with.

"My ideas seem to be so radical and far out in left field that they're totally unacceptable to any of the religious world. But, God, I know I belong to You. I know You love me. And I know You have given me talents You can use . . ."

That was my condition when I returned to Hollywood to work on a TV series. And then in just that flash that evening when I saw all the underground papers—and not a single Christian paper—I somehow knew that here there was something for me.

Strangely enough though, even as I was publishing and distributing that first issue or two of the *Free Paper*, I did not realize . . . the thought never once entered my head . . . that this would turn into the permanent situation as it has. I thought it would be something I would do just that once, or twice, then be back on the road.

But when the responses came back—and my mailbox was jammed with letters from desperate people—I had that same feeling I had in Springfield when I was personally introducing those people to Jesus Christ.

Then the letters came pouring in. And then I knew that God was going to use me to communicate the love of Jesus Christ to those people who were searching. I realized that I had been unsuccessful in communicating with the church people and the religious world.

But now, through His infinite grace and wisdom, He was giving me an opportunity to share Jesus Christ to the rejects and castoffs of society. I felt so humbled . . .

I walked the Boulevard more than one night saying, "Thank You, Jesus. Thank You, Jesus . . ."

Maybe the reason Jesus is using me this way is because I am considered to be a sort of rebel. And Jesus Christ was Himself a rebel . . . in fact, a revolutionary!

Recently while being interviewed for a TV special, one of the men asked me, "Was Jesus Christ a true revolutionary? And, are the Jesus People following His example?"

"The answer," I said, "is yes to both questions. But He wasn't a revolutionary, perhaps, in the sense the word is used today. And the Jesus People aren't revolutionary in the sense that we have any thoughts or plans of violence."

"How, then," he asked, "was Jesus considered a revolutionary?"

"Examples of this are throughout the New Testament," I told him. "For instance, the woman who was taken in adultery, and brought and laid at His feet. The Law of Moses demanded that such a woman should be stoned to death."

"What did Jesus do?"

"Jesus Christ did a revolutionary thing: He forgave that woman," I told my interviewer. "It was unthinkable that mercy should be granted in such an act. But Jesus bestowed mercy.

"Then there was that woman at the well of Samaria. She had lived in adultery for many years. Jesus knew that. Yet, He did not condemn her. He forgave her. He told her of the living water—eternal life—that He wanted to give her. And she, in surprise and gratitude, accepted His offer. Then she ran back to the village—praising God for the new life she had received.

"Jesus' act that day was revolutionary."

I thought a moment before I answered the second part of the question. Then this is what I said, "Yes, the Jesus People are revolutionary—just as Jesus Christ Himself was. The keynote of the entire movement is lifting up Jesus Christ. Not discussing or arguing . . . or getting involved in any particular doctrinal points or views.

"We are called to share Jesus Christ and Him crucified," I said. And I thoroughly believe that.

That's why Jesus People do not "preach" doctrine. Some Jesus People accept and embrace speaking in tongues. Others do not. Some have other views about other doctrines. But as a group . . . as a movement . . . we hold to only one creed: Jesus Christ.

He, alone, is the Way, the Truth and the Light.

He, alone, can bring life to the one who is lost. He, alone, can bring peace and release to the one who was bound by fears and sins.

Jesus Christ was a revolutionary. Because He dared to oppose the ecclesiastical leaders of that day, to open up the windows of heaven—and allow the light of God to shine into a darkened world, and into darkened lives.

CHAPTER NINE

Establishment Reactions

Jesus People seek only to share Jesus Christ. Somehow, this makes them a threat to some people. I don't understand why this is so, except that Satan does everything to prevent this from happening. Consequently there has been some violence directed at some who are sharing the Good News.

For instance, some Jesus People were beaten up in the Spokane and Seattle regions. One boy was talking to some others on the street in Washington state, when they became angry.

"Leave us alone!" one of the youths shouted.

"All I want to do is to tell you that Jesus loves you."

"Outta my way," one man said, "or I'll kill you!"

As the Christian turned to go, one of the young men whipped out a knife and slashed him on the face. He crouched to finish off the Christian, expecting him to run or cry out. Neither response came from the bleeding boy.

Instead, he held his ground and smiled. "Jesus loves you," he said. "And I love you."

The attackers fled.

On the Berkeley campus, several Jesus People were shot at as they sat at a book table. All the shots missed, for which we are very grateful. So far we have not had active persecution in Southern California, but I wouldn't be surprised if this were to come soon. Because Jesus said, "Ye shall be hated of all men for My name's sake . . ."

But even when I've gone to some quite radical meetings in all parts of California, I have always felt great freedom to stand on a bench or trash can and talk to the people. Usually, in the midst of a radical revolutionist speech I find myself some sort of a podium and stand on it. This attracts attention away from the speaker.

Then I say to those around me, "I agree. We've got to have revolution."

Once I have their attention, I go further. "But I challenge you to have a complete revolution!"

"What do you mean?" someone usually asks. "A complete revolution, what's that?"

"I'm talking about real revolution. Total revolution. That's the kind that comes by inviting Jesus Christ into your life."

This stuns them for a minute or so. And while

they're quiet and sort of trying to digest this surprise attack, I say, "There is no other way to change things . . . to really change yourself. Only Jesus Christ can do that."

It's amazing to me that every time I have taken this tack, and have openly shared Jesus Christ as the only way, the only answer, I have gotten an audience. Hundreds of followers at these gatherings seem to listen to anybody who wants to give an answer for the problems they are facing. It isn't so much that most of these people are actively involved in revolution, but that they are actively searching for answers.

So I assure them, "The answer is revolution. And if you want to become part of the real fight, I will show you the way." And as they gather in close I tell them that "The only answer is Jesus Christ . . ."

When I do this, some people have always accepted Him.

Not long ago in Muncie, Indiana, after my lecture, a man got up during the question-and-answer period and asked, "What are you going to do— you and the Jesus People—about all the problems in America?"

As I was getting ready to reply, he went on: "Do not quote from the Bible in your answer."

I said, "It's impossible for me to try to answer you without quoting from the Bible. But I'll try."

"I don't want to hear what the Bible has to say. I want to hear what you Jesus People have to say!"

So I said, "I wish it were possible for me to right all the wrongs that have been done to the black people in America. I wish it were possible for me to right all the wrongs that have been done to the Indians in America.

"I wish it were possible for me to right all the wrongs that were done to the Asians here in America during the Second World War . . . But it's not within my power.

"All we can do is to try to solve the problems of today. Not of the past . . ."

"There is only one real solution to our messed up and confused society," I said.

"That solution . . . the only one that will be lasting and permanent . . . is to change people. And we are working on that. We are out there on the street showing people how they can change. Then, with changed people, we can have a completely changed society.

That wasn't the sort of answer he wanted, so he shook his head and walked away. Then I was able to share Jesus Christ with the rest of the crowd. And many of them were receptive.

It isn't just the so-called radicals, though, who are less than receptive to the Jesus People movement. The Establishment Church, in most cases, is not ready to accept anything so "untraditional" and "orthodox." What so many people cannot see is that the Jesus People are not out to "create a church of our own" or to "change the church"—as much as is our purpose to change men through the power of Christ.

He, then, will do whatever "changing" He deems fit.

Perhaps what we are actually saying and doing can be more effectively described in the words that Paul spoke to the church at Corinth, when he said, "What are you saying? Is there more than one Christ? Was it Paul who died on the Cross for you? Were you baptised in the name of Paul? It makes me thankful that I didn't actually baptise any of you (except Crispus and Gaius), or perhaps someone would be saying I did it in my own name. (Oh yes, I did baptise Sephanas' family, but I can't remember anyone else.)

"For Christ did not send me to see how many I could baptise, but to proclaim the Gospel. And I have not done this by the persuasiveness of clever words, for I have no desire to rob the Cross of its power. The preaching of the Cross is, I know, nonsense to those who are involved in this dying world, but to us who are being saved from death it is nothing less than the power of God" (I Corinthians 1:13-18, Phillips).

The message of the Jesus People has only one note: Jesus Christ and Him crucified. And that is sufficient.

I don't think that anyone of us who are active within the movement even begin to comprehend its vastness. Because, every day we are becoming aware of more things within it—and its outreach, and power—and I begin to see how widespread it really is. Then I stand in awe of what God is doing.

We aren't counting or "keeping score" and trying to nail down numbers. We simply let God do it His own way. We are following Him. We aren't promoting. The Holy Spirit is doing that. We are just trying to do His will . . .

Reactions from the Establishment Church are different. Some like to ignore the Jesus People Movement, perhaps hoping that it will go away. Some actively resist it. A few accept the work as of the Holy Spirit. And these last churches are prospering as they openly allow God to work through them—and in them.

Easter at the Hollywood Bowl.

CHAPTER TEN

Establishment Church Reactions

As I have mentioned before, the Jesus People "uprising" (if you can call it that, and I think you can) has been a completely spontaneous movement. As far as I am able to determine, it began as the Holy Spirit began to work through a gal named Linda Meisner in the Seattle area.

Then from Seattle and the entire state of Washington, it seemed to leap down to the Southern California cities. In fact, at about the same time that Linda began some work in Seattle, Chuck Smith's church opened its arms to the long hairs in Costa Mesa. That was quite revolutionary, and of course there was instant reaction.

It started with just an apartment or Christian commune. I asked Chuck about how it came about.

"Well, Lonnie Frisbee and some of these kids had no place to go. It seemed the Scriptural thing to do was to provide them with food and a place to sleep while we talked to them about the love of Jesus Christ.

"So we rented an apartment—on faith. We didn't have a lot of money. And before we knew it, we had 20 homeless street people living there. It was like wall-to-wall people. They could hardly breathe."

Chuck then rented a house. Within days it was crowded out. So, one at a time, they began opening up other communal Christian houses. And, one by one, they filled up—and during all that time Christ began filling the void in their lives.

"We needed a place to worship," Chuck said, "so we started a Monday night worship service at Calvary Chapel. We had so many long hairs and others who had just come off dope that we knew we had to meet and study the Word.

"Within a few weeks the church was packed out and the people were sitting on the floor. Around the steps to the pulpit. And on the platform itself. I had no place to stand, even. So . . . we opened the church another night . . ."

Now they have Bible rap sessions Monday, Wednesday and Friday—with teaching sessions on the other two nights.

And the reaction was not long in coming.

One of the older "establishment" members

came to him and said, "Chuck, 'they're' coming in and scratching up the pews with the rivets on their levis. And they're getting the carpet dirty with their bare feet. And I don't like it. I don't think it's right!"

So one Sunday morning Chuck brought the problem out in the open. He said, "We'll remove the pews. We'll roll up the carpet. But the street people are staying . . ."

So some of the people got offended and left the church. But the so-called "establishment" people who did stay have now become the real leaders: teaching Bible classes, Sunday school classes, and sharing Christ with a genuine love for people for whom Christ died.

Another strong influence in the Movement is Arthur Blessitt. A tremendously capable person, totally dedicated to the cause of Christ, he goes where the people are—out on the street. Some of his work has brought resistance from the Establishment Church, and publicity from the press. He has the genius of adapting the thrust of his ministry to the ever-changing moods . . . and needs . . . of the people on the street.

On a TV interview recently Arthur told how he operates, and I have seen this happen. "I go into the dirty book stores," he told the interviewer, "and place tracts between the pages of the pornographic material. Now the managers meet me at the door and say, 'Arthur, you are ruining our business. Please stay away.' "

But he doesn't. And God is blessing wonderfully.

One young man in Pasadena felt that the church had missed it, so he began turning on with all sorts of things. This horrified his parents. "But," he told them, "what else is there. I'm not getting turned on by the church . . ."

Then a long hair shared the real Jesus Christ with him and he found reality. Now this high school senior shares his newfound faith openly on the campus. His friends in his church accept him, listen to him. But the majority of the "establishment" people in his church avoid him, raising their eyebrows and shaking their heads. Meanwhile, his parents, having lived through the "disgrace" of having a long hair in their plush, status-conscious home, are beginning to accept this that has happened to their son as genuine, and are cautiously "accepting it" and him.

In a high school underground paper, this boy recently wrote a glowing paragraph in which he said: "It used to be that when I'd score a really good 'lid' the first thing I would do was share it with my close friends. It didn't take long before everyone around me was stoned on it. It's funny, but sad, how fast people would grab a strange stash; but shine on so fast a lifetime with Jesus.

"Jesus Christ came so you could have a life more abundantly; not synthetic junk for your 'head,' but life for your soul!

"If you want to really get into the truth, along with a lasting trip, get your head into Jesus Christ! HE IS ALIVE AND WELL, AND HE LOVES YOU! Glory to Jesus." And he signed his name—along with his telephone number. He really put himself on the line.

Things are happening to the "average" young person in the "average" Establishment Church. Because of the *Hollywood Free Paper* and other underground papers they have begun to see that some of their friends outside the church are getting it on for Jesus. They look around themselves. And what do they see? Well, they often see a plush-carpeted, cushioned sanctuary. They see stained glass windows. They feel the cooling air conditioner. But they see little else.

Often . . . no, usually they see nothing happening. No real warmth. No changed lives. Very little honesty, no concern for the opinions and "way of life" of others.

So what do they do?

Very often they go to the non-church things and get turned on for Jesus.

Then they come back to their "comfortable" Establishment Church and they can see more than before that it's dusty. Sterile. No real life.

These turned-on-for-Jesus youth now must make a decision. They must either get the church turned on. Get something happening within those cracker-box walls. Or, they must go where the action is. Most often, they cannot get their own church turned on.

So they leave. They become part of a regular Bible-rap group. Or a Bible study group that actually gets into the Word of God.

The establishment parents and their Establishment Church are now usually up in arms. Why? Because "the Jesus People have taken our boy or girl from the church." And now that turned on boy or girl seems to "have a mind of his own about Jesus Christ. He will no longer listen to what we have to say about God."

What is the answer?

Certainly not for the street people to forget the whole thing and come down from their high on Jesus, and get back into the same old establishment rut.

The church must make some sort of decision. Because it is the church—not the youth—that is at the crossroads. That's very clear to me: *the church is at the crossroads!*

From here it will either have to (1) forget the whole thing and fold up. Or (2) get it on for Jesus. There is no middle ground.

And so *we actually see both of these alternatives happening.*

I know pastors who have taken one or the other alternative. And I will take a look at them in the next chapter.

"A LITTLE MORE SUGAR, PLEASE"

90

CHAPTER ELEVEN

The Question: Fold Up—Or Get It On?

One of the features I have really appreciated about the Catholic church is that neither the priest or anybody else really cared what you wore . . . or even what you looked like . . . when you went to mass. To worship.

You could be in levis and all set to go fishing the second you split from the church.

You could even walk in with your fishing boots and clothes. And it's at this very point, I believe, that the Establishment Church is beginning to change. To open their arms. To anybody. No matter the length of their hair. No matter what they've got on.

Not all. But some.

Recently I talked with Thom Piper, a good friend of mine, who is associated with Family Counselling Services. He told me that his church and pastor had invited the long hairs into their church, a prominent one in Southern California.

Later I talked with the pastor. "What's happening . . . all the long hairs are coming to your church?" I asked.

He smiled. "Well, at first I didn't know what to do. Then I began listening to our youth. And they said, 'Pastor, this is where it's at.'

"So I began to see that the missionary work isn't all being done in Africa. Or New Guinea. That this is where the action is. And I began a policy of making the church open to these long hairs—especially on Wednesday night."

"And what's happening?"

"It's really exciting. They flock to the front, dressed in about everything you could describe . . ."

"Do they make a disturbance?"

"Not really. They are a bit restless during the first part of the service. You know, during the announcements and all that . . ." He grinned.

"But the moment I open my Bible, things happen. A holy hush falls over this group. You know, they usually sit on the floor in front. Not the pews. But right on the floor in front of me.

"I open my Bible. They open theirs. And, Duane, they are with me all the way. Pencils come out. They mark their Bibles. They take notes. They check references in their Strong's or Young's concordances. You know, the big ones . . ."

"I know, Pastor. I know. The Bible has come alive to them. And you are helping to open it up to them."

He was very serious. "Duane, these street people —Jesus People, or whatever—have made an impact upon my church we will never get away from."

"An impact for good?"

"Yes. For good. And for God. I praise the Lord that I had sense enough to open the doors. And that my people opened their hearts. We are experiencing revival. First Century revival . . . !"

Not all pastors and churches are so open, so wise.

Another large church in Southern California is a case in point. I have worshipped there. In fact, I welcomed the new pastor there when he came.

I said, "Pastor, why did you accept this church?"

He answered, "Duane, I believe that God has brought me here for a specific purpose . . ."

I asked him to be more specific.

"Well," he said, indicating the streets . . . "for instance, these people on our doorsteps. We are doing nothing about them—except to ask them to leave. God wants me—our church—to go out and minister to them."

I looked him square in the eye. "Do you really mean that?"

"Yes. I mean it. That's why I am here."

A week later I got word that this pastor had called the police and reported "those boys across the street from the church." He referred to the street boys who were hustling. And selling their bodies for ten bucks a throw to anybody who would pick them up.

And he told the police, "I don't want that kind of people close to my church. Gives us a bad name."

So I asked myself: "If he had time to call the police, why didn't he have time to fulfill the Great Commission? Why didn't he have time to go across the street and tell these people about Jesus Christ . . . that He loved them . . . ?" I asked myself those questions, and didn't find any answers.

I went back a couple of weeks later. I wanted to ask him.

They had an evangelist in. They were having a "revival." There was just a scattering of people across that huge sanctuary. Practically every person had a pew to himself. And what happened? Nothing. Nothing at all.

And as I was leaving the church, one of the few people who would even touch me asked, "Well, what do you think about it?"

"It gets worse every time."

So as I walked out I spoke to the pastor. I called him by his first name and asked, "Are you *really* doing what God called you here to do?"

He let his eyes brush across me, with no sign of recognition. He turned away. And shook hands with a mink-draped dowager as she walked out.

That was my answer.

I walked out . . . to my "church" . . . the street. The boys were still across the street. Still hustling. Still selling themselves for ten bucks a throw. Nothing had changed.

CHAPTER TWELVE

"I Found It In The Gutter."

A few days ago I got a letter that sounds like so many we get. It was a desperate call for help. It read:

"Man, ya gotta do something! I can't get enough bread to keep me high. I've had some bum trips. I'm all to pieces. The cops are on my tail. My old man kicked me out. If there's anything to this Jesus stuff let me know. Because I've got no chance any other way. I've reached a dead end . . ."

But the thing that got to me is the introduction . . .

It said, "I found this paper in the gutter."

Then we remembered. And as far as we are able to recall—every desperate cry for help has come from a *Free Paper* that they've found in the gutter.

Or on the street. Or in some dirty restroom. Or in some alley. They "found" it.

Doesn't that say something? I'm not sure all that it does say. But for one thing, God is using this discarded, thrown-away *Free Paper* to win the lost to Jesus Christ. God promised that He would honor His Word, and that it would not return unto Him void, ". . . but that it shall accomplish that which I please, *and it shall prosper in the thing whereto I sent it*" (Isaiah 55:11).

All I can say to that is "Praise the Lord!"

One letter that I shall never forget came from a young man in Hawaii. Full of obscenities and four-letter words, this boy cursed God and man with every breath. Nevertheless, the essence of his letter was this:

"I've got a brain tumor. The doctors said I've got only three weeks to live. And the pain is terrible. I can't stand it. All I want to do is get on a high so I can forget what's going to happen. But the pain is so bad I can't get enough bread to keep high. I hate my old man for what he did to me. I hate the straights. I hate everybody. I even hate you, because you said that God loves me. He doesn't! I know that. If He did, why is He letting me suffer like this. I want to get out and surf and drink and have sex. That's all I live for. Can you prove to me that there's a God that loves me? I don't think you can! Last week I slashed my wrists on the beach. Got found by a cop . . . stitches out now . . . Sincerely . . ."

Filled with bitterness and vicious hatred against society and the establishment, the letter ended with obscene curses against God. Through it, though, rang a pathetic cry for help—help that he said he didn't believe existed. Yet help that he was begging to find.

We have been in touch with him through the Movement in Hawaii. I don't know if he's even alive right now. We tried to help him. Maybe we were too late . . .

But—*he found the Free Paper,* and something in it touched off a spark of hope.

Letters like this say to me that God is trying to reach the desperately, almost irretrievably lost men and women. And He is using the *Free Paper* to do it. There is nothing fancy about the paper. It's simple. We ask God to direct us as we write it and lay it out. We ask to direct the artist as he provides illustrations. Then we ask God to send it where it is needed most. And . . . praise His name . . . He is doing just that.

My heart goes out to the street people . . .

To the prostitutes. How much Jesus Christ loved them!

To the drunkards. He wept over them.

To the hated ones of society. He loved them.

To the uneducated ones. He chose His "leaders" from that group.

To the ones who had no hope through the established church. He came to give them hope.

Jesus applied the Old Testament prophecy to Himself where it said: "The Spirit of the Lord is upon me, because he hath anointed me to preach the gospel to the poor; he hath sent me to heal the brokenhearted, to preach deliverance to the captives, and recovering of sight to the blind, to set at liberty them that are bruised.

"To preach the acceptable year of the Lord . . .

"And he begun to say unto them, This day is this scripture fulfilled in your ears" (Luke 4:18, 19, 21).

So, when I get a letter that says, "I found this paper with your address on it . . . in a trash can" or "a dirty restroom . . ." or "in the gutter . . ." I praise God.

Because somehow it is getting out the message to people who have no hope—that Jesus loves them!

And that's what it's all about.

No generation gap . . .

No generation gap . . .

CHAPTER THIRTEEN

Transformations!

Everywhere I go people say, "Tell us some of the 'unusual' happenings you've seen . . ."

My answer is always, "I can't classify any of these things as being unusual . . ."

"What do you mean—not unusual?"

"It's like this. When you recognize the power of the Holy Spirit," I tell them, "and the power which is in the name of Jesus . . . then these things you're talking about are the 'usual'—not the unusual. They are the 'usual' ways God works."

You see, it was that way with the woman caught in adultery. The way He handled that was not usual, but for Him it was the usual. Because He simply showed love.

And with the woman at the well. The one who had been married (or at least had lived with five different men) five times, and was then living with another. Criticism and "preaching" to her wouldn't have done any good. She would have just walked off.

What did He do? He showed her love. He offered her everlasting water that would satisfy her burning thirst.

And she was transformed! She ran back to the village and brought them running to Jesus! "He must be the Messiah!" she said. They came. They heard. And He conquered!

Love did it. Simply love. . . . Love where they were at. He did not invite her to a revival meeting. He brought revival to her right there.

He didn't tell her to find a preacher. He gave her the full message of love right then and there.

Jesus always did that. The time is now! It was in Jesus' day. Even more so in ours.

A few days ago I met a boy from a farm in Kansas. He was living on the Strip. We got to talking.

He said, "Duane, I was doing everything. You know. I was doing everything to get money to shoot up. I was hustling . . . selling myself to anybody . . ."

"What happened?"

"Well, one of the guys on the street began talking to me. And he said something about Jesus loving me."

"What did you think about that?"

"I thought he was putting me on. This Jesus, I told him, couldn't be interested in somebody like me. . . . But he told me that Jesus hung around with the street people. He told me that He didn't care what a person was like . . . that He loved them anyway. He said the reason Jesus came into the world was for people like me.

"So I listened to him. And it sounded good. So we just prayed—right there on the street—and Jesus changed me. Right then. And, you know, Duane. From that moment on I didn't need to shoot up anymore. I didn't need it anymore.

"I came down . . . but I was higher than I'd ever been. I still haven't experienced any withdrawal . . ."

The thing the "straights" (the establishment) can't seem to understand is that the power of Jesus Christ is doing things like that on the street all the time.

Mike came to us recently. His mind was all spaced out. He was 19 and had been on stuff for three years. He told me how all this changed.

"I was at Palm Springs last summer. These guys came around and began witnessing to us. We were up there just having a good time. They began telling us about Jesus Christ.

"Well, I'm a Jew and didn't go for that at first. But after a while it got to me. It was heavy stuff. So, I went into this alley and said, 'Jesus, if You're real, help me.'

"And He did. That's about all there is to it. I haven't blown pot or taken anything since."

The thing I am more and more aware of is this:

the street people don't have to be told they're sinners. They know it. They've done everything there is to do. They've tried it all . . . they've experimented with everything under the sun. They know where it's at. And they want something different.

So when a street person invites Jesus Christ into his life you can see the change immediately. He may still have his long hair. He may still choose to go barefoot. He may still dig his levis.

Yet his bare feet and long hair and his levis don't make him a person (or less of a person, either). The person is on the inside. And that's what is changed. That is what is different about the kid on the street who finds Jesus.

I must tell you about Jeannie. She was raised in the church—went to church and Sunday school all her life. Her father is a minister. She used to sing in church . . . and in revival meetings. But she had never actually known Jesus Christ personally.

Then, just for "kicks" she sang in a night club. From that moment—in only three months—she hit "big time" and the bottom.

"I became a pretty wild entertainer," she said. "A red-hot mama. A singer, dancer, comedienne. I got involved in everything. Drugs, sex, alcohol. I used to drink a couple of fifths of rum a night!

"I got so that unless I was stoned I wasn't happy. Before long I was starring in a show in Vegas. Making $1,500 a week. The devil really got hold of me!"

Then the bottom fell out. She got sick. It started with Hong Kong Flu. Then bronchial pneumonia.

When the doctor told her she had emphysema and cirrhosis of the liver and gave her just two months to live, she was terrified.

Though she was only a young woman, she looked like a very old woman of 75.

"I began crying, 'God . . . God, help me!'

"I was scared that I had committed the unpardonable sin. I knew that God had called me to be a missionary when I was only five years old.

"Now I was in the hospital dying. They scheduled me for surgery. Before I went in I wrote my last will and testament. I called for preachers—rabbis, priests, ministers. All of them. But every time one of them came I was out getting more tests or X-rays.

"I never did get to pray with one of them. I was desperate."

But God didn't let Jeannie down.

And, oddly enough, help came in a most unexpected way. She got a phone call from Chuck, the man who had gotten her started in the mad, endless whirl.

"It was at my lowest point," Jeannie recalls, "that Chuck called me. He sounded different. He told me about how Jesus Christ had completely changed his life.

"At first I thought he was giving me a big line. But, you know . . . he wasn't. And when I realized this, I simply asked that same Jesus to do the same thing for me He had done for my friend Chuck.

"And He did! Praise the Lord!"

Some time later Jeannie asked the Lord to heal

her, which He also did. She is living in San Francisco now. And she is a missionary—a real one—to the street people. She is taking Jesus Christ to the kind of people she was a part of—and understands.

Jeannie was (and is), to put it simply: transformed.

This could go on and on. There are hundreds and hundreds of examples of the tremendous power of Jesus Christ. A couple more I will share, though, which proved to me, personally, how God protects His own people.

It was about two o'clock in the morning. I had just gotten to sleep. Suddenly I was awakened by a banging, splintering noise. I struggled awake to see my door battered down. Someone turned the light on, and about eight or nine members of a bike club crowded into my room.

All of them had been drinking. And all of them were armed with knives or chains.

"Get up!" the leader shouted. He swung a bike chain round and round. I realized that this was no social call.

Somehow, though, the sweet presence of Jesus was with me . . . and I wasn't afraid. I climbed out of bed and just stood there.

All of them were yelling at me. And I couldn't understand at first what they were saying. Except the leader kept shouting, over and over, "I'm going to kill you! Understand . . . ! Kill you! You . . . !"

I felt a strange sense of God's protection. And the words of Ephesians 6:12 came to me—"For we are not fighting against people made of flesh and blood, but against persons without bodies—the evil kings of the unseen world, those mighty satanic beings and great evil princes of darkness who rule this world; and against huge numbers of wicked spirits in the spirit world."

And in the violence and obscenities of those bikers I recognized all that Scripture was describing.

But at the same time I was "strong in the Lord . . . in the power of His might."

It's so hard to put into words the vicious warfare that's present on the street. All—everything—Satan has to offer is there. There are no holds barred. Nothing is sacred. And all of that came to focus in my bedroom that night.

That warfare is very real. I feel that fighting and wrestling with Satan all the time: through the influence of people *he is controlling*. But so many times this fight is even greater at night as I am alone in my room. During the long and often sleepless nights.

My days and late evenings are filled with writing and composing the *Hollywood Free Paper,* plus handling the hundreds of phone calls from people needing immediate help. And immediate prayer.

Besides, there are scores and scores of people who wander from off the street. They come to my office desperately seeking answers to the mystery of life.

It is during those dark hours of night that the toughest battles are won with Satan . . . and I find the victory in Jesus—as I plead with God for the strength I need to go on and to continue the calling that He has placed upon me.

I have never felt adequate for this task. But the battle is the Lord's. I am His. We are both in it together. Praise His name!

That night as I faced those bikers, I felt the demonic power of the underworld. Of hell itself. Yet it seemed that God put an invisible shield between us that they could not penetrate. Finally they calmed to the point where they sat down and became a little more rational.

I told them, "Jesus Christ loves you. No matter what kind of lives you live. No matter. . . . He wants to change you into something real. Something loving . . ."

After a long time they left and I went back to bed.

The next night I got another call from two members of the same bike club.

This time, though, it was different.

They were embarrassed. "We're sorry about last night, Duane. And we came by to . . . to rap about Jesus."

I listened.

Finally one of them said, "Duane . . . what you said about Jesus? I mean . . . does He really love us?"

"Yes, it's true."

"Nobody ever loved me. My old man used to beat me up. I left home. I hit the streets. I was just a punk kid and I was everybody's game. I was scared all the time. Then I got in the club. Now we take what we want. Everybody's scared of us. If we want women, stash, booze . . . whatever . . . we take it.

We're tough . . ."

I just nodded. But I was praying.

He took a deep breath. "Well, what I want to know . . . I mean I'm sick of living like an animal. Is there any way . . . any way out? Can Jesus do anything for me?"

I said, "Yes. If you're willing to give yourself to Him. He will forgive your sins and all your past life. He will make you a new person. Jesus will do all that."

I opened my Bible and read 2 Corinthians 5:17. Then we all prayed. And Jesus Christ transformed these bikers from killers into my brothers in Jesus.

And we saw an immediate change from a hard, vicious attitude—and hate—to one of love and concern for people.

Only Jesus Christ can do that. Praise His name!

Time and again God has reinforced to me the tremendous power in His name—and the transforming power of His presence.

This happened recently when I met Greg.

He was playing a pinball machine in one of the downtown hangouts when I walked up to him. I watched him for a while, then spoke.

"What's happening?"

At first he ignored me. Then he turned and said, "Hi."

We started to talk. I asked him where he was from.

He answered too quickly, "San Diego."

A little later in the conversation, he said, "Well, I really come from San Francisco . . ."

Moments later he said "home" was Salt Lake City.

By this time we were sitting down on the curb, and he began to tell me a story that could only have come out of a book—but which had the sad ring of sincerity that had to be true.

"I'm the oldest child," he said. "My dad's an alcoholic. . . . He used to come home drunk and beat up all us kids. Sometimes he'd grab a butcher knife and tell Mom he was going to kill her. We were all scared of him . . ."

Thought the night was warm, he shuddered. "I ran away from home when I was 13 . . ."

It was my turn to shudder. Before me sat a "mature" 15-year-old who was wise to all the happenings on the street. A boy who knew all that he had to do to survive.

After a while, he sort of ran down. He sat there, his shoulders trembling. He didn't look at me.

Quietly I said, "Greg would you like to pray and tell God all the things you just told me . . . and ask Him to help you? Right now?"

He didn't answer immediately, and I thought he might not have heard me. Then he said, softly, "Yes. I'd like that."

Silence again. Then, a very broken little boy told God the things he had just told me—and asked for forgiveness.

". . . and God, please forgive me for all the wrong things I've done. And, please, God, help me to help my Dad. He really needs You and Your help. Please, God . . ."

That was about all. Then he sighed and looked up, a smile on his boyish face. Somehow the hardness was already beginning to soften. We walked over to our little office on the edge of downtown Hollywood.

On impulse I said, "Greg, would you like to call home?"

He came alive. An excited twinkle came to his lips. "Yes, I sure would!"

I handed him the phone.

As he dialed the number—which he must have thought about many a dark, frighteningly lonely night, I realized I wasn't looking at the same boy I had met only thirty minutes before. But I was looking at a *New Person*. One who had just had his life changed by the tremendous love and power of Jesus Christ.

As the phone was ringing he looked up at me and smiled.

Then he spoke a word that tore at my heart. "Mom . . ."

I could hear the excited shout of joy on the other end of the line. "Greg! Greg! It's you, Greg!"

I realized that any mother in this world would be able to recognize her oldest son's voice—at any time. No matter how often he broke her heart.

"Yes, Mom. It's me." He choked and couldn't speak.

I heard his mother's voice. "Greg. Greg. Are you all right?"

The boy turned his back. I'm sure because he was embarrassed about the tears that began rolling down his cheeks.

"Mom, I'm coming home! I'm all right. I'm different!"

I don't remember much more of that conversation. I guess I was a little misty myself.

That afternoon I shared Greg's story with a businessman. It shook him, too, for he has children of his own.

"I'd like to buy Greg a bus ticket home," I said, "but I don't have the money."

My friend grinned. "Why don't we really surprise his mother," he said, "and fly Greg home today." And he reached in his pocket and pulled out the money.

I have talked with Greg several times since. And his mother wrote to thank me for the part I'd played in his life. "And," she ended the letter, "our whole family is changing . . . because of Greg!"

All I could say was, "Praise the Lord!"

I have thought about Greg and that incident many times. And I know that his mother must have waited long, anxious days and nights for her son to call. She was always waiting. She never gave up hope.

And in just that same way our loving heavenly Father is waiting for His lost wandering children to look up and say, "God, I need You. Will You help me?" And He always does. For He's always there.

No generation gap . . .

Pat Boone and Duane Pederson.

CHAPTER FOURTEEN

What About The Straights?

"Is it possible for somebody other than a street person to reach a street person?"

I hear that question quite often. Especially from the "straights"—those who are not a part of the "street culture" itself.

The answer is, "Definitely."

Because, even though I had been rebellious, I had never truly lived on the streets. Even though 14 years of my life were spent on the road. Most of that time I at least had a car to sleep in.

And, about drugs.

Through a car accident, for which the doctors prescribed some pretty strong drugs to control the pain, I was able to get all the stuff I needed. Until one day I realized I was hooked.

It took a miracle of Jesus Christ to unhook me.

Nevertheless, I have experienced in my own life probably everything the street people have tried. So, in that sense, I was not really a "straight" and God could use me to work with the street people.

But I know of "straights" and "super-straights" who have gone out there on the street—and have shared Jesus Christ. And some of them have communicated Christ's love just as well as anyone else.

I think of one person in particular. He doesn't speak the street language. Yet I have seen him walk up to one of the street people, put his arm around him and say:

"Friend, Jesus loves you."

You ought to see the look he gets—at first. Sometimes he gets rebuffed.

They might shake his arm off and say, "What do you care?"

"I care a lot. I came out here to tell you about Him."

"You mean to tell me that this Jesus loves me?"

"That's right. And he wants to change your life."

Anybody who is filled with the love of Jesus, and directed by the Holy Spirit, can reach these people.

As tough as some of the people are, all they want is love.

As hard as some of the girls are out there on the Boulevard . . . all they are searching for is love.

That's true of all of us.

God made us that way. This desire, this craving for love has got to be filled.

So if you'll go out there and share Jesus Christ . . . and if you're not turned off by the long hair, the bare feet, and even an occasional dirty body that might smell . . . then God will use even you (straight or not) to win these people to Christ.

I think Pat Boone might be classified as a straight. Even though he identifies himself with the Jesus People. I asked Pat about this once.

He said, "Duane, I know I don't live on the street like a lot of these people do. But I love Jesus Christ just as much as they do . . ."

"What does your own church think about your involvement with the Jesus People?"

He chuckled. "They kicked me out."

"Because of the Jesus People?"

"Not entirely. Though I guess it centers around that. They said it was because I believe in modern-day miracles . . ."

"Which you do?"

"Sure. I've seen too many people freed from drugs and diseases not to believe. Something else: I believe in the Holy Spirit. I believe that He can live in a person. And that He can, and does, give power to serve Him."

To his own ability, Pat has been following the Great Commission. I was at his Beverly Hills home one afternoon when he baptized an entire rock band that had accepted Christ.

That was a thrilling day.

While talking to one of the band members, well,

several of them really . . . I asked this one brother what had brought them to Jesus. He pointed to another of the members. "Well, he accepted Christ a while back. Then he came to us and told us he was quitting. We begged him to stay . . ."

He told the band, "Okay, I'll stay till you find someone to replace me. But I'm serious about serving Jesus Christ. And every chance I get I'm going to talk about Him . . ."

The guy I was talking to grinned. "Do you know what he did? He didn't just talk about Jesus. He talked about Him all the time! He acted like he had something so great . . . and, well, one by one he introduced all the rest of us to Jesus."

In his own way Pat is as much a part of the Movement as I am, or Arthur Blessitt, or any other person who is allowing Jesus Christ to work through him, and is reaching out to the ones who don't know Jesus.

Someone else I like to mention again is Lawrence Young. This man is in his sixties, I guess. He is head of counseling at our rock festivals.

Sure the straights can reach street people.

Something interesting to me is this: the Jesus People Movement is reaching a much wider group than just the street people. It is reaching into the Establishment Churches. . . . It is reaching across any and all denominational lines. . . . It is reaching across America. . . . In fact, it is reaching far beyond the boundaries of our land.

This movement of the Holy Spirit is spreading like wildfire. And I believe it is the beginning of the

Left to right: Jack Sparks, Duane Pederson and Linda Meisner.

Arthur Blessitt (left) and Duane Pederson.

most powerful revival in the history of the world.

I don't like to think in terms of setting dates. But I do know that Jesus Christ will not be long in coming. This Movement—this generation—is just paving the way for Him.

To that I say only, "Praise the Lord!"

CHAPTER FIFTEEN

This Is Just The Beginning!

In Disneyland a while back a few of us from the Movement went down to witness during a riot. We invited other Christians to go with us, but they had gone into hiding.

I had several armloads of *Free Papers* with me. I was standing near the entrance, and my friend was filming the action. Just then three policemen stepped up.

"Come with us," one of them said.

"Are we under arrest?" I asked.

"Just come with us," was the only answer we got.

They took both of us into a little room and grilled us.

"What are you doing out there with that dirty underground paper?"

"Sir, we were . . ."

"Answer me! What were you doing out there?"

"Sir, we . . ."

"Shut up! And listen!"

For about an hour and a half they grilled us, accusing us, often with abusive and obscene language, of "Rioting and handing out that dirty paper!"

Each time I tried to answer they told me to shut up, or they ignored me. Finally one of them said, "You don't look like the type to be doing this . . . So, why are you here?"

I began, "Well, we just happen to believe that Jesus Christ is the answer to the problems we are facing today. And we just came down here to share His love with the people who are gathering . . ."

The man in charge turned red and began to stutter some sort of an answer. Then, for the first time, he opened the *Hollywood Free Paper* and began looking at it.

Suddenly he began to chuckle. "Well, it's certainly a different approach! Hmmm! Something I had never thought of."

Then they released us and escorted us off the property. There have been some other confrontations such as this, but not many.

Opposition has come, but usually from a different direction—the Establishment Church. Our mail is sometimes quite heavy, most of it complimentary. But we do get some negative ones. Some very vehement ones. And when these come, almost without exception, they are on the letterhead of one of the major denominations.

For example, once we ran a cartoon in the *Free Paper* which I thought very good. It showed the outside of a factory over which was printed "The Plastic Christian Molding Company." The picture showed all of the little plastic people being dropped out of the mold.

Everybody looked just the same. Hair combed in the same direction, hands at their sides. Long faces. Down in one corner were a couple of long hairs. Someone else in the picture was asking, "Why do you Jesus People look so happy? And why are you so different?"

For some reason, this cartoon bothered a gentleman of the cloth and he wrote a rather blistering letter to complain.

Jesus People seem to get a certain amount of rejection from the Establishment Church, and the establishment world. But, for the most part, they expect that. Because most of them have been rejected anyway.

Our regular rock festivals have been times of great blessing. Times of reaching out to many hungry people who come—some of them—out of curiosity (but remained to pray).

The first festival started in a moment of inspiration. We held it at the Hollywood Palladium, which is just a few blocks from our office. I contacted the man in charge and he showed me the place.

It was so huge . . .

"How many will it hold?" I asked him.

"Four thousand, four hundred."

For a moment my faith was a little shaken. "How much will it cost us?" I asked hesitantly.

He quoted me a price. It sounded astronomical. "But, I'm knocking that down some because you aren't serving liquor," he said.

I thought for a moment . . . then said, "We'll take it."

I went home and began the campaign to fill the Hollywood Palladium. Again God gave affirmation to our plans. He answered our prayers. He supplied the financial means to handle the expenses. But even more important—He once again—through this Jesus rock festival, and others, supplied us with a vital media for getting the papers out.

That very first festival set the pace for ones to follow. We believe the format is God-inspired.

I have always questioned the practice of some evangelistic groups—those who do an entire program before inviting people to Christ. That didn't quite ring true to the Bible. Because the Bible says that "no man can come to the Father unless he is drawn"—and that is God's work, not man's.

I believe very strongly that it is not through cleverness and persuasive words that lead people to Christ. It is the Spirit.

So at the beginning of our festivals (starting with that first one), in about two or three minutes I simply describe the way of salvation. Then I lead the people in prayer.

"If any of you would like to receive Jesus Christ

into your lives," I then say, "please stand . . ."

When people respond, we lead them to counseling rooms and begin sharing Christ with them through our counselors. This is before the program begins. Which means that for however long they may need—even for the entire festival—they can unhurriedly seek and find Jesus Christ.

I am completely convinced that we must work now, for the time is coming soon when we can no longer work. That's why we work tirelessly at the job of spreading the Good News of Jesus Christ.

Presently the *Hollywood Free Paper* is being bulk shipped to every state, and a number of foreign countries. It is being used in the Juvenile Halls of Los Angeles as a "Sunday School paper." Practically every day we get letters and phone calls from people in other parts of the country—asking, "May we reprint the *Free Paper* here?"

Of course we give our permission. The purpose of the paper is to spread the Gospel of Jesus Christ. The *Free Paper* is now only about a year and one half old. By the end of the second year *we believe God is going to enable us to print and distribute over one million copies*—to the glory of His name!

Recently a *Look Magazine* reporter did an article on the Jesus People Movement. It was magnificently done. And, by the way, the writer found Jesus Christ as he wrote the article.

He described how addicts and prostitutes . . . and others . . . are finding deliverance through Jesus. He wound up the article in a wave of glory, climaxing and ending it with these words: "Jesus is coming!"

I believe he was more right than he knew. For the Jesus People Movement—this is just the beginning. I believe it is going to grow and spread, enveloping the entire world in the most tremendous outpouring of the Holy Spirit the world has ever known.

It has already begun . . . and it will continue till He comes!

Praise the Lord! Jesus is coming soon!